The Law of Attraction

Contents

1. Foreword

2. Foreword 2

3. Vibration and The Law of Attraction

4. Connecting the vibes

5. Law of the universe

6. Emotions

7. Focus

8. How to be rich

9. Visualisation

10. Keys to success

Foreword

In 2014 I was sitting in an empty cell in a high secure hospital and this is where my journey began. I wrote down a goal and I am achieving it.

I am a firm believer that the law of attraction has changed my life and without finding the law of attraction I would still be stuck in that empty cell.

I came from an anti-social background, growing up was not easy for me, I was stuck in a system that at the time seemed impossible to get out of. I took the wrong path and my life spiralled out of control. I made countless bad decisions and used my energy in such a negative way.

I can't take back the things that I have done but my energy will never be focused now on the mistakes I have made. When I put my heart in to realising this goal the universe gave me something back! I met Tony Quigley, Ex British super middleweight boxing champion, he believed in me when I spoke and has been where I am trying to get to. Being a patient at a mental hospital and telling people about my beliefs and goals was not easy, but Tony gave me words of wisdom and never laughed at me. I grew as a person in Ashworth, I found my purpose and I now know where I am going. I visualise my goal it will become my reality and I will become everything I want to be.

I want to share with others positive vibrations, just like I felt when I started to embrace the Law of attraction.
I have so many people that have played a part in helping me to change my life, and were there for me in my lowest moments. To all of you thank you.

One of my most special thanks is to Dr Jennifer Killcorn, she knows why, the lady who is late but was always there. To Lucy against all odds, the universe had a plan.

All my bridges are burnt, there is no going back for me. Five years later I am on my way to becoming one of the most entertaining fighters on YouTube.
In 2020 I will be competing, what I am going after is against all odds but I have belief. I visualise my goal, it will become my reality and I will be all that I want to be.

Foreword 2

"I believe success is creating constant pleasure in your life, enabling you to grow"
Ben Hatchett

The Oxford Dictionary definition of the word Knowledge: Information and skills acquired through experience or education.

The word educate has been misguided, its roots come from the Latin word educo, which means to develop from within. To educo – to draw out, to grow through the law of use.

Nature hates idleness in all forms, she gives continuous life only to those elements which are in use. Tie up an arm or any other portion of the body, taking it out of use, and the idle part will soon atrophy and become lifeless. Reverse the order and give an arm more than normal use such as engaging in the gym, working as a builder, then that arm (developed from within) grows strong.

"To become who you are, you must learn who you are"
Pinder – Greek poet

I'm about to get scientific! If you have no knowledge of science then you may find this the boring bit! However it is the most important part, and you should understand this, as it is vital. It is vital to know who and what you are, as well as what everything is, so soldier on through.

The molecule consists of atoms, which are said to be little invisible particles of matter revolving, continuously with the speed of light, on exactly the same principle that the earth revolves around the sun. These little particles of matter known as atoms, which revolve in one continuous circuit, in the molecule, are said to be made up of electrons, the smallest particles of physical matter.
Atoms and electrons revolve round one another at an inconceivable speed.
Every particle of physical matter is in a constant state of highly agitated motion. NOTHING IS EVER STILL, although nearly all physical matter may appear, to the physical eye, to be motionless there is no solid physical matter.

The hardest piece of steel is, but an organized mass, revolving molecules atoms and electrons. In other words the electrons in a piece of steel, are of the same nature, and move at the same rate of speed, as the electrons in gold, silver and other metals. The atom is natures building block, out of which came everything, everything is energy, everything is connected. We are all Vibrations.

Vibrations and The Law of Attraction

Vibrations: the fluid lines that cause the atoms to circle around one another, is a form of energy, which many scientists believe to be of the same energy that we call electricity. However, it is now known to be vibration. The rate of speed with which this force moves, determines the nature of the outward visible appearances of the physical objects in the universe.
The Law of Attraction is all about vibrations. What you focus on is what you get more of (I will focus on that soon)

Psychologists tend to explain it by talking about the reticular activating system, the part of your mind that enables you to filter out most of your environmental stimuli, and only notice those things that seem relevant to your safety, or your highest values. In other words humans automatically and instinctively decide who or what is a threat and who or what they are attracted to.

However many scientists who subscribe to the Law of Attraction theory understand it as we are all energy, magnetic energy that vibrates constantly and will attract whatever frequency we are in tune with.

In music they call this the principle of sympathetic resonance, if you have two pianos in the same room and you hit the C note on one piano you will notice that the C string on the other piano will start vibrating at the same rate. Getting interesting now huh?

I'm glad you've stuck with me past the scientific part! So now you should understand how we work, how we all work.

I want you to think, if everything is made up of energy, what are my vibrations in tune with at this moment? What am I attracting in to my life? What and Who?

Connecting the vibes

"For Whom so firm that cannot be seduced?"
William Shakespeare – Julius Caesar

Do you remember a time when you met someone that you just instantly clicked with? You had so much in common with? Or what about someone you were attracted to? Could you feel the chemistry? The good vibes? What are the vibes? Vibrations! The vibes are the connection!

We are all separate manifestations. We are magnetic energies that connect with other magnetic energies, we desire other manifestations. Think of it as a radio frequency, we receive whatever station we are in tune with, our vibration frequencies are connecting all the time on many levels.

The relationships you have with family and close friends, you can feel the connection there, hence when we lose someone we care for it feels as if you've lost a part of yourself.

These strong connections can be go much deeper, love! That intense energy where your vibrations connect strongly, the love of spending time and being near each other – just like magnets! Mirror neurons play a part here, they were initially noticed in monkeys and later in humans.

Mirror neurons are responsible for humans behaving in the same pattern or mimicking someone after spending prolonged amounts of time with them, gestures, accents, phrases, mannerisms and habits (connecting)

Mirror neurons are present in the parietal and pre-motor cortex of the brain, the areas responsible for movement and attention in the body, mirror neurons show there is a connection between peoples brains, a kind of energy that can fire up another persons brain to cause them to act in a similar way.

This also means the brain can communicate with external forces (energy).

It's a horrible feeling to lose someone you love, all the words used to describe and explain that feeling 'hole in my heart' 'lost' etc. They all refer to being broken, that the connection is broken, your magnetic energy is incomplete.

It takes time to fill that void, repair and feel better.

Love and sexual relationships open up another channel for discussion as People separate for many reasons, one of those reasons, I believe is that a person can start to evolve in a different direction, your thoughts start sending different vibrations, with different vibrations come different frequencies, you can develop other manifestations of desire.

Emotions can and do change, 40-50% of marriages end in divorce, the average UK marriage lasts just eleven and a half years, it's also important to remember that just because people are married doesn't necessarily mean they are happy. I won't put the statistics for adultery (they're not good). Why? Is probably the question we should be asking.

Marketing is a great metaphor for this question – The world is full of marketing, if you were to walk in to a supermarket and everything was in plain packaging completely unbranded and the prices were all the same, unless you were to open everything you were going to purchase and smell and taste to separate what you did and didn't want to purchase you'd most likely just grab whatever was nearest!

Marketing companies advertise and target individuals to buy their product, the ways they do it either visual or vocal is the same principle with attracting people, people market themselves and when one buys the same product for a long time it can become boring and easy to start noticing other brands with better appeal.

Wouldn't it be natural for temptation and curiosity to start creeping in? Think how many people are in the world? Now think how many of them you would be compatible with? How many would share your interests, feel a chemistry, be in tune with the same vibrational frequency as you?

I'm not saying this is the case for every couple, I believe there are many high vibrational super magnetic couples going strong. However what I am saying is, as humans we are constantly evolving.

Law of the universe vs. Laws of society

Nothing has meaning except for the meaning we give to it ourselves
T.Harve Eker

Laws of the universe and the laws of society are two different laws, you should remember that. Man created society, man did not create the universe. Let's use the partners cheating for an example- it's socially perceived and believed to be wrong. Why? Is it not internalization instead of inclination? (This may sound as if I'm an advocate for cheating, which I'm not)
We believe it to be wrong, because that's what we've learnt growing up, it becomes part of our value system.

This is further supported by social norms, normative influences such as positive expectations of others.
It is normative influence that leads to public compliance, when you're driving along the road and you come to traffic lights if its red you know to stop, amber is a warning and green is go. You know and believe this because you've been programmed to.
We learn through observation (mirror neurons) in the late 1970's Albert Bandura carried out a social learning experiment, Bandura divided a group of young boys and girls from a nursery school.

Individually, the children would go in to a playroom where there were toys and an inflatable Bobo doll (a cheery looking clown), in each case an adult walked in to the room and played on their own with the toys for a minute, with the child watching.

The adult would behave either kindly towards Bobo for the remainder of their time in the room or take the toys and start to administer the clown with a good whacking. Now, when the adult left the room, all eyes were on the behaviour of the children. Those who had seen the adult play gently with the clown followed suit, giving it the same loving, playful attention. However the children who had seen the adult treat Bobo badly made a different choice.

They mimicked the adults by playing with the toys, but only using them as weapons to give poor old Bobo another bashing! It's important to realise when we're being influenced. TV news, the papers, they all use social influence. Mostly propaganda, using loaded language to produce an emotional, rather than rational response to the information being presented.

Politicians use loaded language all the time to further their agenda. The words are chosen carefully, Charles Stevenson noticed, that there are words that don't just describe a possible state of affairs. "Terrorist" is not only used to refer to a person who commits specific actions with specific intent. Words such as "torture" or "freedom" carry with them something more than a simple description of a concept or an action.

Words have a magnetic effect, an imperative force, a tendency to influence the recipient's decisions. They are strictly bound to moral values leading to value judgements and potentially triggering specific emotions. For this reason, they have an emotive dimension. In modern psychological terminology, we can say that these terms carry 'emotional valance' as they presuppose and trigger a value judgement that can lead to an emotion.

Emotions

"Success trains, failure complains" - YouTube

What are emotions? Emotions are a habit, you get what you tolerate. You get used to tolerating that feeling, then you start thinking that feeling's me! When actually it's not, it's a habit. Habit is the language we use, the way we look at the world.

The language we use affects us, it affects the brain, it's like a muscle when you go to the gym, you can, and need to train it. You can train yourself to be frustrated all the time, by doing it all the time! You can train yourself to be stressed out or sad, the more we do something the more wired we become in doing that something.

White matter, is developed in the brain when we learn new skills, we can create and develop new white matter endlessly, this begins with the myelination stage developing pathways that stick together and strengthen over the practice period, when the time comes something remarkable happens the white matter strengthens around the myelination that then send 100 x faster impulses, this makes doing a skill effortless.

Like I said the good news is we can develop new white matter, so you can train yourself to be passionate, strong, you don't need to settle for the emotions you've got, motive does matter! (see what I did there with the matter #justsaying)

I'm not saying that we won't feel crappy and down at times because we will, hormones and other chemicals in the brain play a part in this, but it's about learning how to pull yourself out of that place, focus on positivity.

Focus

"Your brain is like Google, ask it questions and it will search for the answers"
Ben Hatchett

What we focus on is what we look for, if we ask ourselves negative questions such as "why always me?", "why do they get on my case?", "why does this happen to me?", then the brain will search for the answers. Negative questions equal negative answers. Your brain will find memories relating to your questions and then trigger the relating emotions.

So what if we ask ourselves questions such as "Why am I so lucky?" " How am I so lucky?" our brains will search for the answers looking for positive memories linked to luck, therefore focusing our emotions towards positivity. The questions we ask determine how we feel.

Mental state = Feel = Focus = Behaviour

The only experience you have of life comes in two forms. How you are feeling physically, because of the condition and use of your body at that given moment. In other words if you have physical pain then that's obviously going to affect your mental state. When you haven't slept look at the effect it has on you, when you have a high in sugar/caffeine food or drink, these alter our physical state.

The other thing that controls your state is what you are paying attention to. Let's say, for example, think of the colour green, now look up and look for green, you will notice more things that are green that you would have before because that is where your attention is.

If you're feeling crappy you're not going to do so well, now I know there are exceptions, but those exceptions are because you control your focus, because you don't focus on feeling crappy you focus on what needs to be done.

There is tremendous power in the focus of your mind, if you want to look at the quality of your life and know what it is – it's the quality of the state you live day by day, isn't that really true? Is it how you feel day to day that determines how you treat yourself? How you treat other people? How great or how poor you feel about your life is determined by how you treat your body.

Develop new habits, reflect on how you focus. There are two important words one should consider WANT and HAVE, the definition of Want being should or need to do something, lack being short of something, desirable or essential, lack of deficiency – poverty – wanter. Look at the words that describe want, they're not exactly the most enthusiastic are they?

Now the other word is have = has, having, have got, be able to make use of, refuse to tolerate. The haves and the have – nots.

Look at the difference in the words. A lot of people want, "I want this" or "I want that" but they rarely do anything about having what it is they really want, it's easy to talk about everything you want, true character comes from using the word have, "I am going to have the things I want" do not put your energy in the idea of wanting things, instead put it in to "how can I have" there's a huge difference.

"It is not the critic who counts, not the man who points out how the strong man stumbled or where he could have done better. The credit belongs to the man who is actually in the arena; whose face is marred by dust, sweat and blood, who strives valiantly, who errs and comes short again and again, who knows the great enthusiasms, the great devotion, and spends himself in a worthy cause, who at best knows in the end triumph of great achievement, and who, at worst, if he fails, at least fail while daring greatly, so that his place shall never be with those cold and timid souls who know neither victory nor defeat."

Theodore Roosevelt (1858-1919)

How to be Rich

'Risk only comes from not knowing what you are doing'
Warren Buffet

It all comes down to yourself, and what you want to put your mind to, if you want to be rich, then put yourself in tune with it, don't just want it, believe you have it, go commit. We have the internet, look at YouTube, it's free education, there are talks and lessons that years ago you would have had to pay to attend.

Don't be afraid to read (and finish) books, so many wealthy successful people all say that making money is a skill just like any other, and as we now know when we learn a new skill we develop white matter, which we all have and we can always develop.

As Conor McGregor says "There is no such thing as talent, it's hard work and determination" making money is never easy, if it was everyone would do it! But the fact is everyone could if they truly believed and didn't let life turn them in to being inauspicious.

It's easy to believe that we don't have the intelligence, but how do we measure intelligence? Intelligence is a measure of the number and quality of distinction that you have in a given situation. For example, if you talk to Eskimos you find out that they have more than a dozen words for the word 'snow' More than a dozen! I'm from the sunny coastal town of Eastbourne, how many words do you think I know for snow? One and that's snow!

But Eskimos need to make more of a fine distinction to be effective in day to day life. They need to know what snow they can make an igloo out of, what snow they can take their dogs through, what snow they can eat, and what snow they can fall through. So who has more intelligence and power in the snowy environment? The Eskimo or me? The Eskimo of course!

Now if an Eskimo came to Eastbourne driving around with me, he would not know where to go or how to navigate his way about the town. He would not know how to go shopping. So in that situation it would be me who had the necessary skills to survive. Who has the intelligence then? Your intelligence is your knowledge in a given situation, you have the power to choose your situations or at least the power to control how you respond to these situations.

Visualization

'What the mind believes, the body can achieve'
Napoleon Hill

Roger Banister was the first person to run the four minute mile when for centuries people had been trying. How? He didn't just physically practice, he made a shift in his head, he practiced in his head, because he could never achieve this just physically, so he had to change his thought process first, then his body would get him through. After Roger ran that four minute mile within the space of two years after 37 other people did it.

Potential –Belief - Action – Results

Here's how it works, the potential is always there for what you want, depending on whether or not you tap in to your own potential, it is to do with the action you take, and this will determine the results you get. Most people already have a belief about their potential which affects the action they take, of course this affects the results, then ironically the results reinforces their belief.
If you believe there is little potential, how much action are you really going to take? Nothing......a little maybe, then when you get little results, what does this do to your belief?

The mental state to aim for is that of absolute certainty, "This is going to work, I know I'm going to make this work, I will find a way" with this mindset you're going to tap in to a lot more potential, you take massive action, when you really believe in something, you get great results. When you get great results your brain goes "See I told you this would work out" now you have an even stronger belief and even more potential.

It all comes from self-belief, from believing in yourself with every fibre of you're being.

Keys to success

You must have a definitive purpose. A definitive purpose must be accompanied by a definitive plan, followed by appropriate action. If the action isn't working, you can always change the plan of action, but you must always be sure of the purpose. What is your purpose?

1. Write a clear description of your desire in life, what position will you accept for success? Remember your only limitations are those that you set up in your own mind, or those that you let others set up for you.

2. Write a clear statement of what it is you're willing to give to get what you desire.

Have Faith in yourself, you are powerful, believe and you will achieve.

Lightning Source UK Ltd.
Milton Keynes UK
UKHW021817220822
407649UK00008B/1577